All about Misty Copeland

INCLUDES FACTS, INSPIRING QUOTES, QUIZZES, ACTIVITIES AND MUCH, MUCH MORE.

ISBN: 978-1-83990-421-9

LULU AND BELL: 2024

This Book is an unofficial book and is not authorized, sponsored or endorsed by Misty Copeland.

Fact File

MISTY COPELAND

From: Kansas City, Missouri

Zodiac Sign: Virgo

DOB: September 10 1982

FUN FACTS:

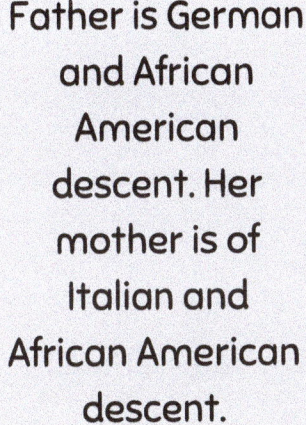

Father is German and African American descent. Her mother is of Italian and African American descent.

1. She is the youngest of four children.

2. As a child she would often dance to songs by Mariah Carey.

3. She loves reading books.

MISTY

FUN FACTS:

1. During middle school, she became captain of the drill team.

2. After three months of studying ballet she was en pointe.

4. She moved in with her ballet coach and her family to be closer to her ballet classes.

She began her dance career learning ballet at the San Pedro Dance Center aged 13.

Copeland never studied ballet or gymnastics until her teenage years.

At aged fourteen she won her first sole role and national ballet contest.

I KNEW THAT I JUST DIDN'T HAVE IT IN ME TO GIVE UP, EVEN IF I SOMETIMES FELT LIKE A FOOL FOR CONTINUING TO BELIEVE.

MISTY COPELAND

At fifteen she won first place in the Los Angles Music Center Spotlight Awards.

FUN FACTS:

1. In 2000 she became a member of ABT's studio company.

2. She became an ABT soloist in 2007.

3. One of the youngest ABT dancers promoted to soloist.

In 2015, she became the first African-American woman to be promoted to principal ballerina in ABT's 75 year history.

When she was younger her role model was Nadia Comaneci after watching the film Nadia.

She appeared in Prince's music video for the cover of 'Crimson and Clover' in 2009.

FUN FACTS:

1. She toured with Prince.

2. She started acting lessons in 2009.

3. She enjoys cooking.

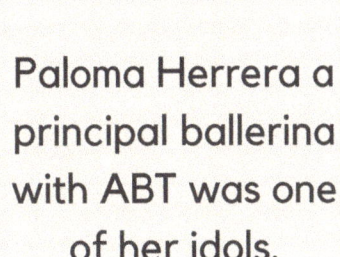

Paloma Herrera a principal ballerina with ABT was one of her idols.

I MAY NOT BE THERE YET, BUT I AM CLOSER THAN I WAS YESTERDAY.

MISTY COPELAND

FUN FACTS:

1. In 2011 she appeared in an episode of A Day in the Life.

2. In 2015 she appeared on the cover of Time magazine.

3. She didn't own a computer until she was 22 years old.

She struggled to find ballet slippers that matched her skin colour, so she dyed her own.

In 2014 she became the first black woman to play Odette/Odile in an American Ballet Theatre production of Swan Lake.

SHE ENJOYS EATING PIZZA

FUN FACTS:

1. She performed in the Broadway production of On the Town.

2. She has released two children's books called Firebird and Bunheads.

3. She loves horror movies.

Copeland danced the role of lead ballerina in the 2018 Disney film The Nutcracker and the Four Realms.

In 2014 Barack Obama added her to the president's council on Fitness, sports and nutrition.

Decide what you want. Declare it to the world. See yourself winning. And remember that if you are persistent as well as patient, you can get whatever you seek.

MISTY COPELAND

She helped set up Project Pile which trains dance teachers in racially diverse communities.

She has appeared as a guest judge for the 11th season of So You Think You Can Dance.

In 2017 Copeland published the book Ballerina Body sharing the message about body positivity.

She is an advocate for body positivity.

Be strong, be fearless, be beautiful. And believe that anything is possible when you have the right people there to support you.

MISTY COPELAND

Create your own design

Create your own design

Create your own design

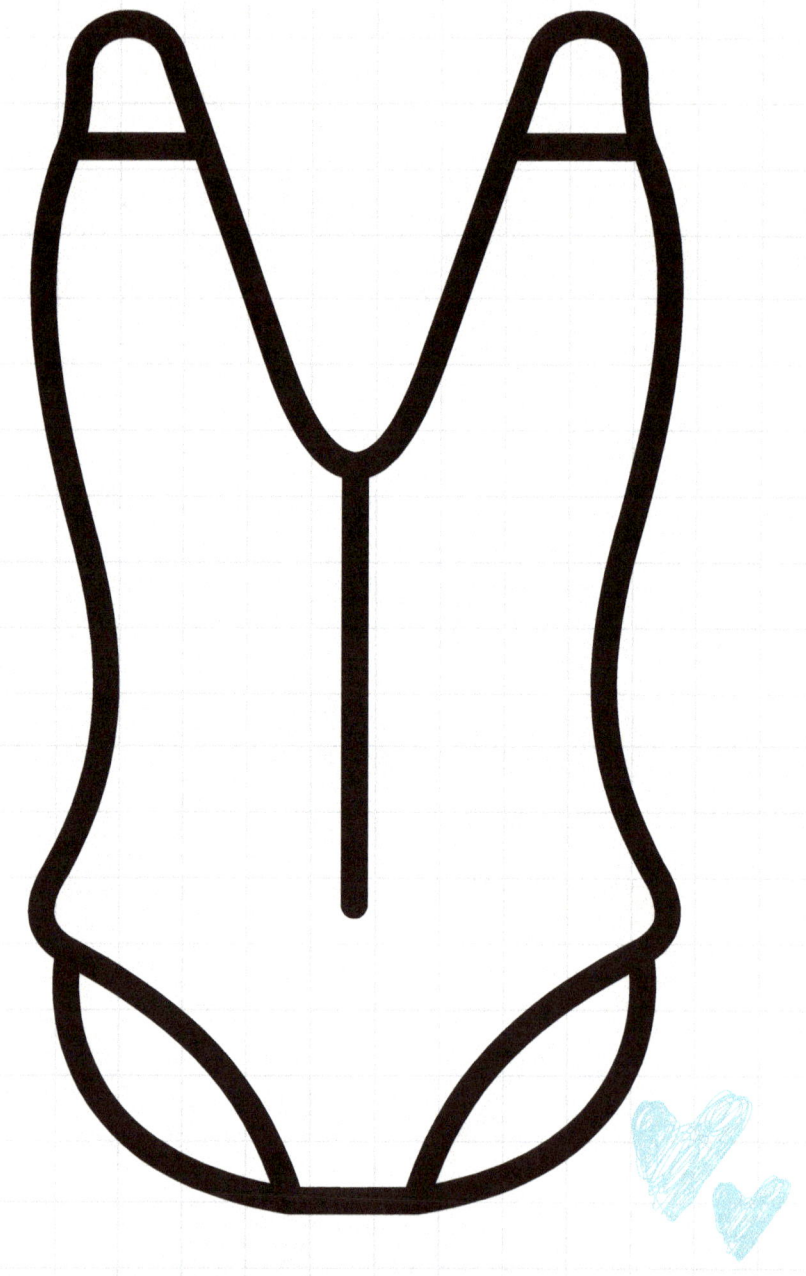

Belonging shouldn't mean you are like everyone else.

— MISTY COPELAND

WORDSEARCH

Find and circle the words.

B	S	B	A	L	L	E	T	E	S	A	M	S
A	W	A	E	R	R	C	Y	T	H	M	R	I
L	A	T	I	P	I	R	O	U	E	T	T	E
L	N	H	W	G	M	R	D	T	W	E	N	P
E	L	E	F	S	O	T	A	T	S	R	I	I
R	A	R	S	T	R	E	T	C	H	U	J	L
I	K	R	E	E	N	H	G	R	S	E	U	E
N	E	N	K	R	T	E	H	J	T	R	M	I
A	Y	M	I	Y	J	E	T	G	E	E	P	L
N	U	T	C	R	A	C	K	E	R	O	I	E
K	A	E	R	I	A	L	R	K	Y	A	N	S
M	I	S	T	Y	C	O	P	E	L	A	N	D

- ballet
- pile
- ballerina
- Misty Copeland
- pirouette
- stretch
- jump
- nutcracker

KNOWING THAT IT HAS NEVER BEEN DONE BEFORE MAKES ME WANT TO FIGHT EVEN HARDER.

MISTY COPELAND

Colour me in

Colour me in

Colour me in

Colour me in

Don't underestimate yourself. You are more capable than you think.

— MISTY COPELAND

HOW WELL DO YOU KNOW MISTY COPELAND?

What year was Misty Copeland born?

A) 1981

B) 1982

C) 1980

D) 1985

HOW WELL DO YOU KNOW MISTY COPELAND?

What age did Misty Copeland start learning ballet?

A) 10

B) 12

C) 15

D) 13

HOW WELL DO YOU KNOW MISTY COPELAND?

Which musical artist video did she appear in?

A) Prince

B) Beyonce

C) Stevie Wonder

D) Taylor Swift

HOW WELL DO YOU KNOW MISTY COPELAND?

What Disney film has she appeared in?

A) Beauty and the Beast

B) The Nutcracker and the Four Realms

C) Sleeping Beauty

D) Cinderella

HOW WELL DO YOU KNOW MISTY COPELAND?

What was her 2017 book called?

A) Ballerina Story

B) The Ballet Dancer

C) Misty Copeland

D) Ballerina Body

HOW WELL DO YOU KNOW MISTY COPELAND?

Answers

B) 1982

D) 13

A) Prince

B) The Nutcracker and the Four Realms

D) Ballerina Body

You can start late, look different, be uncertain and still succeed.

MISTY COPELAND

NOTES

NOTES

NOTES

NOTES

NOTES

NOTES

NOTES

NOTES

NOTES

www.ingramcontent.com/pod-product-compliance
Lightning Source LLC
Chambersburg PA
CBHW041311110526
44590CB00028B/4318